digging deeper **3** BRITAIN 1750–1900

ALAN BROOKS-TYREMAN JANE SHUTER KATE SMITH

Heinemann

Heinemann Educational Publishers
Halley Court, Jordan Hill, Oxford, OX2 8EJ
a division of Reed Educational & Professional Publishing Ltd
Heinemann is a registered trademark of Reed Educational & Professional Publishing Ltd

OXFORD MELBOURNE AUCKLAND
JOHANNESBURG BLANTYRE GABORONE
IBADAN PORTSMOUTH NH (USA) CHICAGO

© Heinemann Educational Publishers 2000

First published 2000

ISBN 0 435 32773 9

02 01 00
10 9 8 7 6 5 4 3 2 1

Designed and produced by Gecko Limited, Bicester, Oxon

Original illustrations © Heinemann Educational Publishers 2000

Illustrated by Mike Spoor and Geoff Ward

Printed and bound in Spain by Mateu Cromo

Photographic acknowledgements
The authors and publishers would like to thank the following for permission to reproduce
photographs:
Cover photograph: © Bridgeman Art Library

Bridgeman Art Library: pp. 33, 52; British Museum: p. 37 (bottom); Leeds Central Library:
p. 48 (top); Mary Evans Picture Library: pp. 5, 18, 20, 24, 29, 41, 45, 46, 48 (bottom), 53,
56, 57; National Archives Washington: p. 22 (right); National Army Museum: p. 30;
National Galleries of Scotland: p. 23 (top); National Library of Australia/Rex Nan Kivell:
p. 62; National Portrait Gallery: pp. 7, 16/17; Norfolk Rural Life Museum: p. 23 (bottom);
Post Office: p. 43; Ronald Grant Archive: p. 36; Royal Photographic Society: p. 25.

Written sources acknowledgements
The authors and publishers gratefully acknowledge the following publications from which
written sources in the book are drawn. In some sources the wording or sentence has been
simplified.

Peter Haining, *The Mystery and Horrible Murders of Sweeney Todd, Demon Barber of Fleet
Street*, Muller, 1979: 37D; 38F, G, H, I.

Thomas Shapter, *The History of the Cholera in Exeter in 1832*, S. R. Publishers Ltd, 1971:
32, A, B.

The publishers have made every effort to trace the copyright holders but if they have
inadvertantly overlooked any, they will be pleased to make the necessary arrangements at
the first opportunity.

CONTENTS

HISTORICAL SKILLS

DIGGING DEEPER

THEMES

Cross-referencing primary sources
The slums of London and Manchester

'It's true! I read it in a book!' No good student of history would think about using such a comment. It is important to be critical of everything that we read. When looking at sources, it is a good idea to question their strengths and weaknesses. One way of deciding whether a piece of information is likely to be reliable is to see whether it can be found in other sources. If it can, it is more likely to be a fact. This is called 'cross-referencing'. We are going to look at a range of primary sources about the living conditions of the poor in two mid-nineteenth-century cities – London and Manchester.

London was the capital city and a large working-class area had existed for a long time. Manchester was one of the new industrial towns where there had been rapid and widespread building of cheap housing for factory workers. There were established middle- and upper-class areas in both places. The people who lived there avoided contact with the working-class areas as much as possible. This was mainly because they were afraid of disease, and seeing how bad living and working conditions could be.

SOURCE A

In Whitechapel, London, there is no water laid on to any houses. The people get their water from a well in the courts. The result is a scarcity (shortage) of water. When they are washing clothes the smell of the dirt mixed with soap is most offensive. This must have a very bad effect on people's health. There is no such thing as a sink for getting rid of water!

From Edwin Chadwick's *Report on Public Health*, 1842. Many of the people who had gathered the evidence were afraid to publish it because it named and shamed private water companies. Chadwick took full responsibility for the publication and distributed over 10,000 free copies to people in power such as politicians and journalists.

SOURCE B

In the first house that I turned into there was a single room; the window was very small and the light came in through the door. The young woman there said, 'Look there at that great hole; the landlord will not mend it. Either my husband or I have every night to sit and watch, because that hole is over a common sewer and the rats come up twenty at a time, and if we did not watch for them they would eat the baby up.'

Description of Frying Pan Alley in London taken from a reported interview given by Lord Shaftesbury in 1847. He was a leading reformer, and had already introduced laws to change conditions in the factories in 1833 and in the mines in 1842.

SOURCE C

The room, though two or three feet higher than the door, is so low that the head of the tallest of the visitors would touch the blackened ceiling if he stood upright. It is offensive to every sense; even the gross candle burns pale and sickly in the polluted air. There are a couple of benches only in the room. The men lie asleep where they stumbled down (because they were tired or drunk), but the women sit by the candle.

A description of a London slum from the novel *Bleak House* written by Charles Dickens.

An engraving by Gustav Doré called Bluegate Fields c. 1870. It shows a street in a poor area with a central sewer. This caused killer diseases.

SOURCE E

The houses have broken windows and moisture creeps up the walls making them black and damp. The walls crack, the roof leaks and many of the doors and windows do not fit. The houses are the last refuge between poverty and death. Below the miserable dwellings are rows of cellars. Twelve to fifteen human beings are crowded into each of those damp holes.

From *Journeys to England and Ireland* by Alexis de Toqueville, a French nobleman. In 1835 he visited Manchester and was shocked by what he saw.

SOURCE F

Many of the houses are old, dirty and too small. Masses of refuse, **offal** and sickening filth lie among stagnant pools of water; the air is poisoned by the smell of muck and darkened by the smoke of a dozen factory chimneys. A group of ragged women and children swarm here and they are as filthy as the pigs that live amongst the rubbish tips and refuse. The whole rookery (slum) is a disgusting sight.

From *The Condition of the Working Class of England* by Frederick Engels, a German socialist and close friend of Karl Marx. He wrote this description after visiting Manchester in 1842.

Shepherd's Buildings consist of two rows of houses with a very narrow street between them. The houses are built back-to-back. The privies (toilets) are in the centre of each row. Over them is part of a sleeping room. There is no ventilation in the bedrooms. The cellars are let out as separate dwellings; these are dark, damp and very low. In the centre of the street is a common (shared) open gutter, into which all sorts of refuse are thrown. In many of these houses there are four people in each bed.

This description was written by William Rayner, Medical Officer for Stockport, a town near Manchester. It formed part of a government inquiry carried out between 1839 and 1842 into living conditions in large towns.

Work it out!

1 First, it is important to identify what the sources are saying. List the facts included in each source, and then see if they can be found in any of the other sources. One has been done for you. Copy the chart and continue to tick which sources back up the points listed. Then do the same for the other sources.

2 Using the charts you have just made, state what similarities you can find between the conditions described in London and those described in Manchester. Why do you think there are these similarities?

3 Are there any differences?

4 Look at Source C. It was written by a great fiction writer, who knew London and had visited the slums. He was famous for his detailed and highly colourful descriptions of people and places. His dramatic stories were written as a serial for a weekly newspaper. Explain why you think this source might be **a)** unreliable **b)** reliable.

5 Using the information that you consider to be most reliable write a paragraph describing poor housing in London and Manchester.

6 From this evidence would you expect living conditions for the poor in other newly industrialised towns to be similar? If so why?

7 If you were a member of the government enquiry in 1842, what improvements would you recommend should be carried out and why?

Source F (Manchester) Supported by Source	A	B	C	D	E	G
Houses dirty	✓				✓	
Refuse						✓
No drains				✓		✓
Smell and polluted air	✓		✓			

Putting evidence in context
An interview with Octavia Hill

The nineteenth century was a time of great social reform. Some of the famous reformers were:

- Lord Shaftesbury who introduced laws to change working conditions in factories and mines
- William Wilberforce who campaigned against **slavery**
- Robert Owen who worked to improve working conditions in the factories and set up the first national trade union
- Edwin Chadwick who was appointed to help to solve the problem of what to do with the poor.

These important reformers were all men. The following sources and information are about the work of a woman social reformer. Octavia Hill came from a privileged (wealthy) background, but used her position and education to help the poor.

SOURCE B

About four years ago I bought three houses in one of the worst courts of Marylebone, London. Six other houses were bought subsequently (later). All were crowded with families. The first thing to be done was to put them in decent order. The area last purchased was a row of cottages facing a bit of waste ground, occupied with wretched, broken-down cow-sheds, manure heaps, old timber, and rubbish of every description.

The houses were in a shocking condition; the plaster was dropping from the walls; on one staircase a pail was placed to catch the rain that fell through the roof. All the staircases were perfectly dark; the banisters were gone, having been burnt as firewood by tenants. The dustbin was often emptied by boys who spread nasty objects over the court. The state of the drainage was as bad as everything else. The pavement of the backyard was all broken up, and great puddles stood in it, so that the damp crept up the outer walls.

From Octavia Hill's book *Homes of the London Poor* (1875).

Biographical details

Octavia Hill (1838–1912) came from a wealthy background and was the grand-daughter of Dr Southwood Smith who had been a social reformer and promoted the 1842 Public Health report. She was determined to establish good quality housing at fair rents for the poor. From 1864, with the help of a loan from the artist John Ruskin, she bought up old slums and made them into pleasant homes. She believed that parks and open spaces in cities were essential and was co-founder of the National Trust in 1895. She described what she saw and her ideas for reform in her books *Homes of the London Poor* (1875) and *Our Common Land* (1878).

SOURCE A

A portrait of Octavia Hill.

Sources C and D are extracts from *Homes of the London Poor*. Octavia Hill is describing who lived in her houses, what she did to repair them and some of the rules she laid down for her tenants.

SOURCE C

As soon as I entered into possession, each family had an opportunity of doing better; those who would not pay, or who led clearly immoral lives, were thrown out. The rooms they left were cleaned; the tenants who showed signs of improvement moved into them. The drains were put in order and a large slate water tank was fixed. The roof, the plaster, the woodwork was repaired; the staircase walls were painted; new grates were fixed; the layers of paper and rag (black with age) were torn from the windows, and glass was put in; out of 192 panes only eight were found unbroken. The yard and footpath were paved.

A slum house. Study the drawing and decide what you think Octavia Hill would have wanted to improve, based on what you know of her from the evidence in Sources B and C.

SOURCE D

The rooms, as a rule, were re-let at the same prices at which they had been before; but tenants with large families were advised to take two rooms, and for these much less was charged than if let singly. No sub-letting is permitted. The elder girls are employed three times a week in scrubbing the passages (corridors) in the houses. For this work they are paid, and by it they learn habits of cleanliness.

Work it out!

1 You have been asked to interview Octavia Hill. Use the biographical details and the sources to think of questions to ask her about her aims, work and achievements. Then find the answers. To start you off:

Interviewer: 'Octavia Hill, it is a pleasure to meet you. May I ask why you have bought houses in one of the worst **courts** in Marylebone?

Octavia Hill: ....

Interviewer: 'That is very interesting. Could you describe the houses when you bought them?'

Octavia Hill: ....

Interviewer: ....

Using the evidence, produce a list of questions you would wish to ask her. These might include: 'What are your rules for your tenants?' or 'Would you evict (throw out) someone from your homes?'

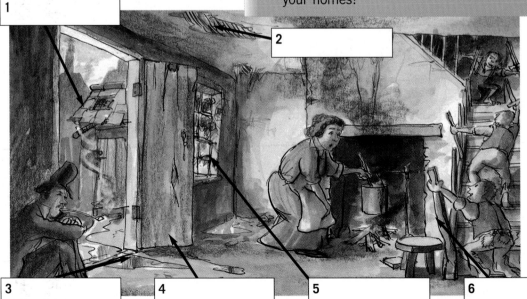

1
2
3
4
5
6

Using oral testimony
Factory children

Since the beginning of the 1800s people's awareness of the working conditions in many factories was beginning to grow. In 1802 laws were passed to ban night work and set a maximum ten-hour shift for apprentices, but since there was no one to enforce these laws they were ignored. The 'Ten-Hour' movement (to limit working hours for children and adults to ten hours) grew throughout the 1820s, its leaders particularly emphasising the treatment of children to gain public support. One reformer, Richard Oastler, wrote pamphlets comparing factory conditions with slavery.

In 1831, the evidence collected by a Parliamentary Committee into working conditions in factories shocked the public. A Royal Commission was set up to supply the government with more information. Sources A – D give an idea of some of the evidence given to the commissioners.

SOURCE A

The girls aged seven and nine go to the mills at three o'clock in the morning and finish work at ten in the evening ... my eldest daughter when she first went there, the cog caught her fingernail and screwed it off (her finger) below the knuckle. She was five weeks in Leeds Infirmary and her wages were stopped. With being so tired, she was frequently beaten.

It was near eleven o'clock before we could get them into bed after getting a little victuals (food). We have cried often when we have given them the little food we had to give them. We had to shake them, and they have fallen asleep with the victuals in their mouths many a time.

Samuel Coulson's account of children at work given to the Government Commissioner for the Royal Commission of 1832.

SOURCE B

The Government Commissioner asked: 'How are the children in the factory treated?'

The answer came:

– 'They are generally cruelly treated; so cruelly treated, that they dare not hardly for their lives be too late at their work in a morning. When I have been at the mills at seven o'clock in the winter season, when the children are at work in the evening, the very first thing they inquire is, "What o'clock is it?" They look so anxious to know what o'clock it is, that I am convinced the children are fatigued, and think that even at seven they have worked too long. My heart has been ready to bleed for them when I have seen them so tired, for they appear in such as state of insensibility (cannot think or act) as really not to know whether they are doing their work or not.'

– It was explained that 'the children were beaten to keep them awake: some were beaten so violently that they lost their lives in consequence of their being so beaten'.

SOURCE C

An illustration from Frances Trollope's novel *The Adventures of Michael Armstrong, Factory Boy*, written in 1840. She describes factory conditions, and Michael started work at the age of six.

'Before this committee there passed an endless procession of broken human beings. Joseph Haberjam, aged seventeen years, described his day's work when he was seven. He began at five a.m and cndcd at eight p.m with half an hour off for a meal at noon.

"What means were taken to keep you at your work so long?"

"There were three overlookers (men who controlled production); there was one kept on purpose to strap." (i.e. to beat the children)

"How far do you live from the mill?"

"A good mile."

"Was it very painful for you to move?"

"Yes, in the morning I could scarcely walk, and my brother and sister used out of kindness, to take me under each arm, and run with me to the mill, and my legs dragged on the ground; in consequence of the pain I could not walk…" The children are frequently sick because of the dust and dirt they eat with their meal.'

The evidence of Joseph Haberjam given in 1831. He received 2s 9d (13p) a week for his 14½ hour day at the age of seven.

REGULATIONS

Fines

Any spinner found with his window open.................................**1s**

Any spinner found washing himself...**1s**

Any spinner leaving his oil-can out of its place **6d**

Any spinner found whistling **1s**

Any spinner being five minutes after last bell rings **2s**

Any spinner being sick and cannot find another spinner to give satisfaction to pay for steam per day **6d**

These 'Regulations' appeared in a Burnley cotton mill in 1852.

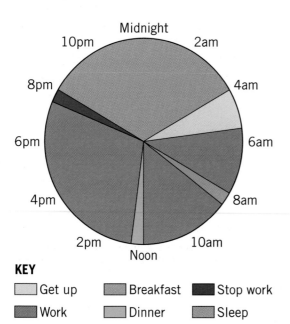

KEY

- Get up
- Work
- Breakfast
- Dinner
- Stop work
- Sleep

The working day in a Lancashire cotton factory.

A doctor's opinion on children in Manchester cotton mills, 1832:

The children leaving the Manchester cotton mills appear to me almost universally ill-looking, small, sickly, barefoot and ill-clad. Many appeared to be no older than seven. The men, generally from 16 to 24 were almost as pale and thin as the children. The women were the most respectable in appearance.

Dr Turner Thackrah wrote this about children working in a Manchester cotton mill in 1832. We have to remember that this is the account of one doctor in one particular factory.

The factory owner's point of view

- Shorter working hours would mean less production, fewer goods to export and less money.
- Britain would lose her position as the world's leading industrial producer.
- Injuries happen when workers lose concentration – it is their fault.
- Children are beaten at home or in the factory otherwise they would become lazy and have no respect.

The Factory Act of 1833

Following the findings of the commission into factory conditions, Parliament passed a new law in 1833 called the Factory Act. Here are some of its recommendations :

Hours of work

- Children under nine years old not to work in textile mills
- Children aged nine to thirteen to work no more than nine hours
- Young people aged fourteen to eighteen to work no more than twelve hours
- No one under eighteen to do night work

Government inspectors

Four inspectors were appointed by the government to make sure that factory owners were keeping the law.

Work it out!

1 Do you think that the government commissioners would have been given truthful answers to their questions? Explain your answer.

2 Would the government commissioners' report have been welcomed by

  a the factory owners
  b the factory workers
  c the government?

In each case, support your answer with a quote from the primary sources.

3 Write a report on children's working conditions in factories from the evidence you have.

First you need to collect the information for your report. Copy the following headings and write down quotations from all the sources under each one:

- Age the children start work
- The hours they work
- Time off for meals/sleep
- Injury
- Exhaustion
- Strictness of the rules

Now use the writing frame (on the right) to help you. Remember, each paragraph starts with a main idea, followed by supporting details.

4 Read the information box on the Factory Act of 1833.

  a From the evidence that you have read, what criticisms would you make of the new law?

  b With the knowledge that you have about factory conditions, produce a set of recommendations designed to improve conditions for children and adults in the factories.

REPORT ON CHILDREN'S WORKING CONDITIONS

I have been investigating the working conditions of children in the textile factories.
I have heard evidence from three people.

Children are very young when they start their working lives. For instance ....
....

The children are very cruelly treated.
For example, children .... (include punishment, working hours and meal times).

There is evidence that the health of the children is damaged ....(include injury, pain, tiredness and death and illness, sick pay).

The factory owner believes that these conditions are necessary for him to make a profit. He has argued ....
....

11

Autobiography – a good historical source?
Testing Olaudah Equiano's story

A portrait of Olaudah Equiano.

Some background details of the life of Olaudah Equiano

Olaudah Equiano was born in the Kingdom of Benin in Nigeria. He was the youngest child of the family and was kidnapped with his sister. He became separated from her during the journey. In 1757 when he was only twelve years old, Equiano arrived in London. Between 1757 and 1762 he served on board several ships. While in Greenwich, he met the Guerin sisters who sent him to school for a brief period between ships. He finally bought his freedom from his last master, Robert King, in July 1766. He never saw the abolition of **slavery** but contributed to the debate through his autobiography and writing to newspapers. His writing also challenged the view held by many, that Africans were illiterate and therefore inferior.

SOURCE B

I was soon put under the decks where, with the smell and my grief, I became so sick that I was unable to eat. For not eating I was beaten. I would have jumped over the side of the ship but I could not. The crew watched us closely. The stench (stink) of the hold, the heat and the crowding, which meant that each had scarcely room to turn himself, almost suffocated us.

There was sickness among the slaves of which many died. The situation was worsened by the rubbing of the chains and the filth of the lavatory buckets into which the children often fell. The shrieks of the women and the groans of the dying gave the whole a scene of horror.

I became so sick that, as I was a young boy, my chains were removed and I was allowed to stay on deck. One day, two of my countrymen who were chained together, preferring death to such a life of misery, jumped into the sea.

From the autobiography of Olaudah Equiano.

SOURCE C

At last we anchored off Bridgetown (in Barbados). Many merchants and planters (plantation owners) came on board and examined us attentively. They also made us jump. We were penned up like so many sheep. We were sold. In this manner relations and friends were separated, most of them never to see each other again.

I and some few more slaves that were not saleable were shipped off to Virginia, where I was sold to a planter. I was exceedingly miserable as I had no person to speak to that I could understand.

I was horrified to see in the kitchens a black woman slave who was cruelly loaded with various kinds of iron devices. She had one particularly on her head which locked her mouth so fast that she could scarcely speak and could not eat nor drink.

A second extract from Olaudah Equiano's autobiography.

Work it out!

Use the writing frame here in order to produce a piece of extended writing. In the first section, you will examine how reliable the source is, and in the second section you can explain how the source can be tested.

1   **Olaudah Equiano's autobiography is an excellent historical source. He clearly describes conditions on board ship.** Use Source B to continue writing the paragraph.

2   **He describes the experience of being sold into slavery.** Use Source C to help you with this.

3   **In his autobiography, Equiano tells us a little about how slave workers were treated.** The final part of Source C will give you the information that you need.

4   **The sources are also important because Equiano expresses his and other people's emotions. He helps us to understand his feelings when he entered the ship and was sold into slavery. We understand more than just the bare facts.**

5   **However, when we study history, we need to question the sources. This is only one person's account of being a slave. We need to cross-reference this information. It may be possible to find out more about Equiano.........** Use the background details to explain how you may continue your research on the author.

6   It is also possible to check the autobiography against other sources. **From Source D, we know that there is other evidence.** (Use the picture and caption to explain this). **It is estimated that between 1700 and 1784, 600,000 slaves arrived in Jamaica, therefore, other evidence must exist such as ....** (give examples and explain why).

Finally, write your conclusion. Explain what you think about the value of Equiano's autobiography as a historical source.

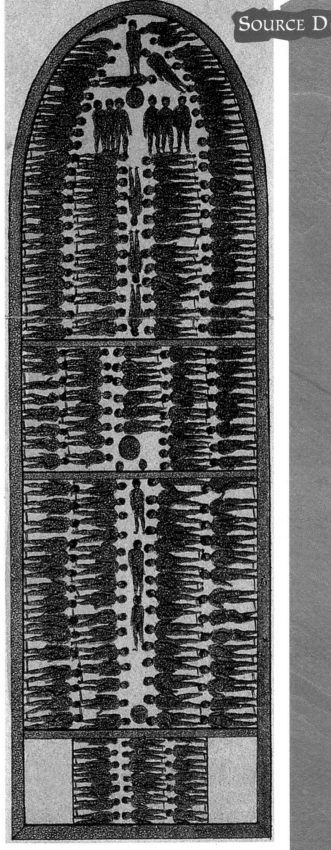

SOURCE D

A plan of how slaves were packed into a ship, from a book written by Thomas Clarkson, an anti-slavery campaigner.

Using pictorial evidence
British attitudes towards the Empire

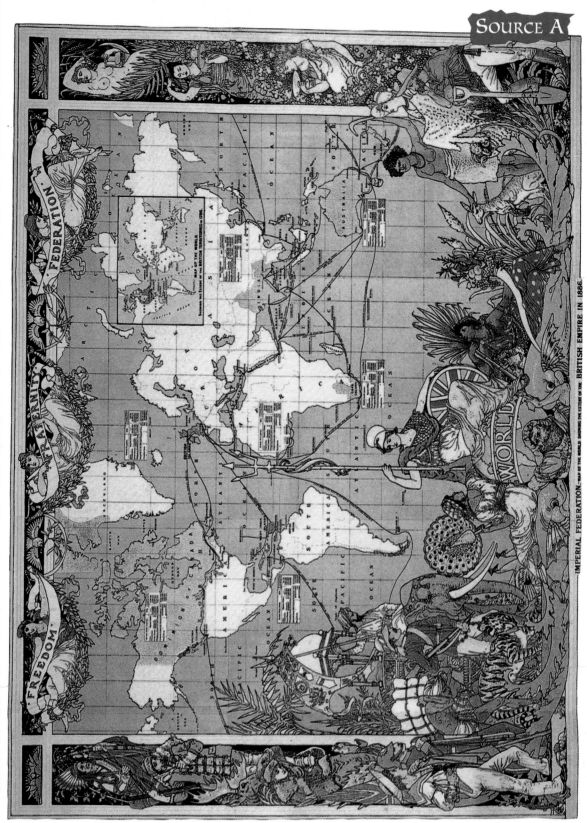

A map of the 'Imperial Federation', 1886.

Reading maps as a source of historical evidence

Maps were sometimes drawn and decorated to tell a story or put out a message, rather than to show accurate geographical detail. This map of the world (Source A) has some areas shown in the colour pink. These are the lands the map shows to be ruled by Britain in 1886. At the top of the map, there are three words 'Freedom' '**Fraternity**' and 'Federation'. Around the map, there is a border showing some of the different peoples who were governed by Britain. At the bottom of the border, in the centre, there is the symbol of Britannia sitting on top of the world supported by Neptune, the god of the sea.

SOURCE B

Muv (mother) taught history from a large illustrated book called *Our Island Story* with a beautiful picture of Queen Victoria at the front of the book. 'See, England and all our Empire possessions are a lovely pink on the map', she explained. 'Germany is a hideous, mud coloured brown'.

The illustrations, the text, and Muv's comments created a series of vivid scenes …. The heroic Empire builders, fighting for the glory of England …. The Americans, who had been expelled from the Empire for causing trouble and who no longer had the right to be pretty pink on the map ….. the good so good, and the bad so bad, history as taught by muv was on the whole very clear to me.

Jessica Mitford describing her childhood in the 1920s in her autobiography *Hons and Rebels*, published in 1960.

Work it out!

1 Look carefully at the map and the detailed drawings round it. Do you think this map is likely to represent an accurate geographical picture? Give reasons for your answer.

2 Look up the meanings of the words: 'Freedom, Fraternity and Federation'. From your definitions, explain the message behind the map.

3 Study the border round the map.

  a Try to identify some of the people and where they come from.

  b Symbols were used at the time of Empire to represent certain countries. Find and identify as many as you can.

  c How do the symbols explain the British attitude at this time to the countries of the Empire?

  d Why do you think the map has a border like this?

4 The source shows that Britain gained its Empire through its navy and sea power. Identify the images that could be used to back up this statement.

5 Why do you think that this map was produced in this way?

6 Do you think British people of the time were proud of their Empire? Use the evidence in the map in your answer.

7 What can be learnt from Source B about British attitudes towards the Empire?

8 Do you think the attitudes expressed in Source B are similar to the attitudes expressed by the producer of the map in Source A? Explain your answer.

Reading paintings

Artists sometimes paint a picture in order to tell us a story or let us know about certain attitudes and values held at the time.

Six people appear in this painting.

On the left:
Prince Albert, *husband of Queen Victoria* (1819–December 1861)

Lady in waiting *unidentified*

Queen Victoria (1819–1901)

On the right:
Viscount Palmerston *Prime Minister* (1784–1865)

Lord John Russell *Foreign Secretary* (1792–1878)

An unidentified African chief

Queen Victoria presenting a Bible at Windsor Castle, painted by Thomas Jones Barker in 1861.

Understanding the evidence

This is a good historical source for explaining the Victorians' relationship with the Empire. It also tells us something about Victoria and Albert. The painting is full of symbolism. Use the following questions to help you understand what the artist was telling us.

1 Who is the most important person in the picture?
2 Who is the least important?
3 Why was Albert there? How do we know that Victoria was seen to be more important than her husband?
4 The Prime Minister and the Foreign Secretary were there – what does this signify?
5 Why does the artist use the colours red, white and blue so much?
6 Why do you think we do not know the identity of the African chief?
   What does he represent?
7 Why is Queen Victoria presenting a Bible to the African chief?
8 What does the Bible tell us about the relationship between England and Africa?
9 Describe the expressions and attitudes of all the characters. How does this help to tell us about the relationship between England and Africa?
10 Having studied the painting carefully, and answered the questions, write a paragraph describing the scene and explain what it tells us about British attitudes to empire in the Victorian period.

Work it out!

1 Look at the dates of the people present in the painting.

   a Could all of them have been together?

   b Was it likely, given their roles, that they would have been together at Windsor Castle?

2 What other sources might be used to find out whether the ceremony shown in the picture really happened?

3 Explain whether you think the painting is of an actual event or whether it is symbolic.

Historical enquiry
Advances in medicine

Throughout history smallpox has been a killer disease. In the eighteenth century it was thought to have killed 40,000 people a year in England. The disease started with a high temperature and headaches. After four or five days, a rash developed on the victim's face, feet and hands. The rash turned to blisters about a week later. Many people died as a result of the disease. Those who were fortunate enough to survive were left with pock marks (scars where the blisters had been). Others became blind or deaf.

Vaccination (producing the disease in a mild form so that the patient would be immune to further infection) had already been practised with some success, but it was not until Jenner, working as a country doctor, discovered that inoculation with the cowpox vaccine would prevent smallpox, that this disease was diminished in many countries. His methods led to similar methods being developed to deal with other killer diseases.

SOURCE A

Edward Jenner.

Edward Jenner

Edward Jenner (1749–1823) had discovered that milkmaids who had suffered from a mild disease known as cowpox were proof against smallpox. He decided to carry out an experiment in which an eight-year-old boy was deliberately infected with 'vaccine', a preparation of pus from the sores of a milkmaid suffering from cowpox. Once the boy had recovered from the disease Jenner injected him with smallpox. As Jenner expected, the boy did not catch smallpox. He had been 'immunised' against the disease by having already had cowpox. Jenner called this process vaccination and is widely credited with having invented a treatment which helped wipe out killer diseases.

In the long European wars after the French Revolution, five or six million human lives were lost. In Europe, vaccination has already preserved from death a greater number of human beings than were sacrificed during the course of these wars. The work of Jenner saved far more human lives than the sword of Napoleon destroyed.

The British government spent millions of pounds on these wars and freely gave honours and large annual pensions to wounded soldiers. But it grudgingly rewarded Jenner with just £30,000 for saving 30,000 people every year.

Sir James Simpson, writing in 1847 about the importance of Jenner's work.

Sir James Simpson

Sir James Simpson (1811–70) was a world-famous doctor from Edinburgh, where there was a well-established medical school. In 1846 he discovered the use of chloroform as an **anaesthetic**, and went on to make advances not only in anaesthetics, but also in **gynaecology** and **obstetrics**. He was a member of almost every medical society across Europe and America, wrote extensively about his work and other interests, and when he died was given a public funeral and recognised as one of the great men of medical history.

Work it out!

When we are finding out about the past, we have to ask questions. Under the following headings are lists of questions that need to be asked about that topic. When you have worked out some answers to these with the help of the chart below, you should be able to write about the whole subject in your answer to the extended question.

Smallpox

a) What was it? b) What were the symptoms? c) What was vaccination? d) Was it a very common disease? e) Was it a fatal illness?

Edward Jenner

a) Where did he work? b) What was cowpox? c) What did he notice about cowpox? d) How did he decide to try to prove his theory? e) What was this process called?

The results

a) Did everybody believe Jenner's research? b) Was he rewarded for his work? c) How successful was his work? d) Could the same process that was used to protect against smallpox be used to fight other fatal diseases?

1 Copy and complete the chart below in order to:

a find as many answers to the questions as you can from the sources and information

b identify the questions that cannot be answered from the sources and information

c suggest what sources of evidence you would use to answer these questions. Where would you find these sources?

2 Some people have called Jenner 'the father of vaccinations'. What do you think they mean by this? How would you find out whether his work really was important in the history of medicine?

Question	answer	no information here	what to look for
Smallpox a) b)			

Historical evidence
The cartoon

The Cow Pock – or – the Wonderful Effects of the New Inoculation. James Gillray produced this cartoon to show that at the time that Edward Jenner was developing a vaccine against smallpox, there was widespread suspicion and ignorance of inoculation. Some people believed that if they volunteered to have the vaccine, they would acquire 'cow-like' features…look at the right-hand side of the picture!

James Gillray – Cartoonist

James Gillray (1757–1815) first became successful around about 1784 and published about 1,500 cartoons. He was extremely cutting and rude. Politicians tried to buy his services so that he did not produce work showing them in a bad light. Gillray produced arguably 'the most elaborate political cartoon ever published' (see Source C). It is generally agreed that Gillray was mad for the last four years of his life. He made suicide attempts and was protected, as far as possible, by his publisher, Hannah Humphrey.

On Wednesday afternoon, Mr Gillray the Caricaturist (cartoonist)… attempted to throw himself out of the window of his attic room. There being iron bars (at the window) his head got jammed! The incident was observed from White's (Club) and assistance was given to the unfortunate man.

From *The Examiner* newspaper, 21 July 1811.

SOURCE C

This cartoon by Gillray is called 'The apotheosis (deification or making god-like) of Hoche'. It was published in January 1798. General Hoche had just died, and is rising from the post-revolutionary France of Napoleon into an extraordinary revolutionary heaven.

Work it out!

When studying cartoons, it is important to place them in context. Sometimes it is not possible to find out the exact answers to the questions that we need to ask:

- What do we know about the person who produced the source?
- Why was it produced?
- Was that person an eye witness?
- Who did the cartoonist expect to see the source?

1 Look at Sources A and B and try to answer the questions listed above. From your knowledge do you think that Gillray was giving an accurate impression of current attitudes in the cartoon in Source A?

2 Look at Source C. In the centre of the painting is the French General Lazare Hoche. Do you think that Gillray sees him as a hero or a villain?

3 The cartoon is a wild collection of images. It is also very controlled using a mathematical theory. Look at the 'ten commandments' in the centre of the picture. What does this tell us about Gillray's attitude towards Hoche?

Changing the way we look at the past

In 1839 the first cameras were invented. People being photographed had to stay very still for several minutes, otherwise the picture would be blurred. Some early photographers fixed a metal neck brace to their sitters' heads to keep them still! From the very beginning they gave us a very different way of looking at the past. Before 1839, any pictures of the past were artist's impressions – paintings for people to hang on their walls or engravings in newspapers. In both cases a person looked at something and then drew it for other people to look at. Photos let people look at the real thing.

First photos

Modern cameras take photos that are very quick to take and develop. Polaroid cameras can print pictures straight away, and digital cameras can transfer an image straight on to a computer. Early photos were nothing like this! They were either black and white, or had to be coloured by hand.

The person who produced Source A obviously copied the photo in Source B. It was drawn for a magazine article on **slavery**. The artist tried to be as accurate in his copying as possible. It is clearly the same person, in the same pose, with the same pattern of scarring on his back. But Source B has more impact on people. It is a real person.

SOURCE B

SOURCE A

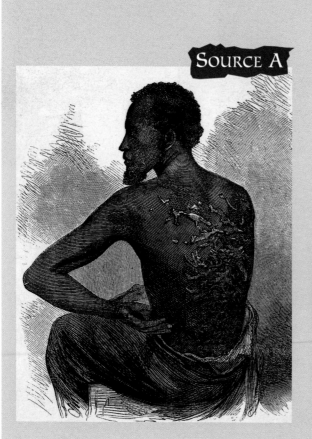

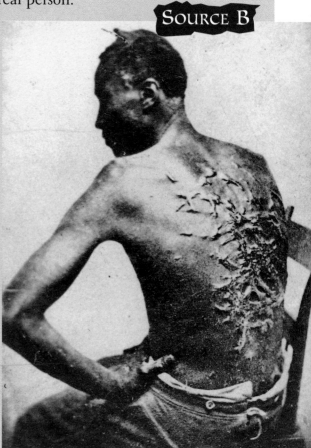

A late Victorian painting of potato planting in the spring.

SOURCE D

A photo of potato harvesting, taken a few years after the death of Queen Victoria.

Work it out!

1 Which of Sources A and B would you use if you were writing an anti-slavery pamphlet?

2 How similar are sources C and D?

To answer this question consider the following:

a Are they showing the same thing like sources A and B?

b What are the workers doing?

c What impression does each source give of the work?

3 a Why do you think the artist painted Source C?

b How might that affect the way he showed the scene?

4 a Why do you think the photographer took Source D?

b Does the fact that it is a black and white photo have an effect on the impression you get from it?

5 Which of the two sources gives you the best idea of what it was like to be a farm worker?

23

Photos did show real people. But they did not always show real situations. From the very beginning, photos were posed for effect. Photographers very quickly developed ways to make 'trick' photographs. Even when a photographer was not making a trick photo, he or she could still be taking the photo to prove a point to make people think a certain thing. You have to look at a photo and ask yourself why it was taken before you accept what it is showing you.

SOURCE E

Why did they take it?

Photographers took photos for many reasons. Some took pictures of people or places (especially foreign places) to show what they looked like. These people had the least reason to make a photo show anything but what was there.

Some people took photos to tell a story just as a painting did. These photos could be of family scenes or farming scenes or even, as in some cases, schoolroom scenes. They are all carefully posed. People do not get in each other's way, or look smudged because they have moved. These were sold as 'art', like paintings.

Other people took photos for a social purpose. The charity **Barnardo's** took 'before' and 'after' photos of the children they took in, fed and housed and found work. Many of these photos were not true before and after photos, the photos were taken to encourage people to think that Barnardo's was doing a good job, and should be given money to help carry on.

Just for professionals?

At first cameras were heavy. It also took a long time to take and develop photos. But camera technology changed rapidly. In 1888 the American George Eastman produced a camera that was simple to use. His slogan was: *You press the button and we'll do the rest.* Now everyone could take photos.

This photo is an obvious example of a trick photo. Fairies of course, do not exist. The photo was made by using two layers of film, one with the fairies painted on to it.

24

Helping artists?

Many artists began to use photographs to help them in their work. W.P. Frith's famous painting of Paddington railway station (see page 52) was painted with the help of photographs of the station taken by a friend of his. These helped him to get the details of the building exactly right. He still painted the people from real-life models in his studio. Other painters, such as Tissot, used photos of family groups as a basis for their paintings. They changed the position of people to make the painting more 'artistic'. They had to remember or invent the colours, but they used the photo to make a painted record of an exact moment in time.

Work it out!

1 a How do we know Source E is a trick photo?

  b Does the artist mean to trick us into believing that fairies really exist?

2 Does the fact it is set up mean the photo doesn't tell us anything useful?

3 a What does Source F show?

  b Do you think it was set up, or not? Explain your answer.

4 Source F was, in fact, a photo made by using several layers of film. The girl in white was actually lying in bed, dying of consumption. The photo shows her with her family in their front room.

The Zulu war

During the reign of Queen Victoria Britain steadily took over more and more lands in other countries, building up a huge Empire. Sometimes the takeover was peaceful. Most often, it was done by force. The British army grew in size and skill and travelled widely as the Empire grew. From the 1850s onwards, the army was usually fighting in at least one part of the world.

Africa was the 'new continent' that was being opened up by explorers and then taken over by various European countries.

The Victorian view of Africa was simple. It was big, rich in resources and empty – apart from the simple, savage natives who lived there. These savages would benefit from the British takeover. They would be 'civilised' by the British. The army would crush any initial resistance from the African peoples.

Southern Africa was a focus for British expansion after diamonds were found there in 1871. The British moved steadily north. They took land from African tribes and from white settlers (originally Dutch) called Boers.

The Zulu kingdom was a collection of tribes led by a king. They were in a fairly constant state of border 'push-and-shove' with neighbouring countries. When the old king died, in 1872, a British officer crowned the new king, Cetshwayo, to stop anyone else claiming the throne. In 1877 a new governor, Sir Bartle Frere, was sent to southern Africa, fresh from 'civilising' India. Frere was convinced that Zululand had to become part of the Empire. To gain support for this, he emphasised the strength of the organised Zulu army, which he called 'a frightfully efficient manslaying war machine'. He created a dispute with Cetshwayo as an excuse to invade Zululand.

In January 1879 the British army invaded Zululand. The war that followed was short, but bloody. Two very different armies, with very different skills and equipment, met in a war that each side wanted to win quickly, in open battles. So what were the two armies like?

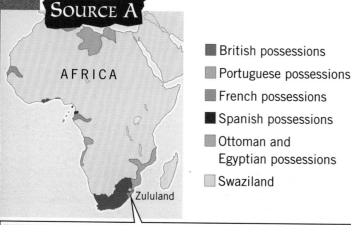

SOURCE A

AFRICA

■ British possessions
□ Portuguese possessions
■ French possessions
■ Spanish possessions
□ Ottoman and Egyptian possessions
□ Swaziland

Zululand

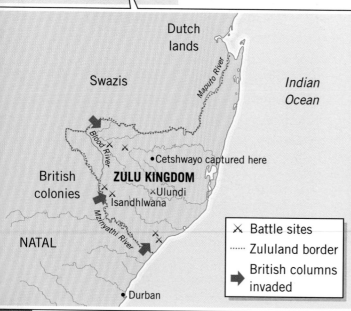

Dutch lands

Swazis

Maputo River

Indian Ocean

Blood River

×Cetshwayo captured here

British colonies

ZULU KINGDOM

×Ulundi

×Isandhlwana

Mzinyathi River

NATAL

× Battle sites
····· Zululand border
➤ British columns invaded

• Durban

Map of Zululand and surrounding countries.

The British army

- 18,000 soldiers, 5,500 regular troops, the rest natives from Natal or white colonists
- army highly trained and organised
- uniforms were heavy and very visible
- armed with: rifles, gatling guns and other firepower
- did not know the ground, had maps, but they were not very accurate
- had to bring in own supplies and weapons on wagons
- slow moving, moved in groups, with supplies, at the pace of the slowest wagon

Chelmsford's plan

Chelmsford, the British army commander, wanted to make an example of the Zulus. He wanted to show all the African nations that the British army was best, so there was no point resisting them. This meant that he had to beat them quickly and decisively. He underestimated their skill and determination and expected that after one or two battles the British would win. After all, they had the firepower and the skill to use it.

The Zulu army

- 24,000 soldiers, all Zulus
- army highly trained and organised
- light clothing
- armed with: spears, knives and shields
- on own ground, knew the country
- could get food supplies from people
- fast moving

Cetshwayo's plan

Cetshwayo had tried and failed to get other African countries to support him against the British. While the strengths of his army might make a long-drawn-out guerrilla war look the best bet, he decided against this. Firstly, his army were warriors and did not approve of 'sneaky' guerrilla tactics. Secondly, a long-drawn-out war might weaken his army, and they might then be attacked by their neighbours, as well as the British. Thirdly, he hoped that the British would make peace if they saw that the Zulus were hard to beat.

Work it out!

1 Plan a debate between various Zulu leaders about the best way to fight the British. Think about the strengths and weaknesses of the Zulu army, as well as the strengths and weaknesses of the British army.

2 Why do you think the British underestimated the Zulu army?

SOURCE B

Zulu warrior   British soldier

The war

Chelmsford sent in his army as five separate columns. Their orders were to advance on, and capture, the Zulu capital, Ulundi. The British won the first few skirmishes easily.

Isandhlwana: the first battle

The British centre column, about 4,700 men, camped below Isandhlwana hill on the night of 20 January. Scouts failed to see the 24,000-strong Zulu army camped just over a nearby hill. The Zulu plan made full use of the fact that they knew the ground and where the British were, while the British had no idea of the size or location of the Zulu army.

A Zulu group let a British scouting party spot and follow them. They lit fires along the ridge of a hill, to seem like the main Zulu camp. The British fell for the trick and sent for reinforcements. Early on the morning of 22 January, the reinforcements set out. They left behind just under 2,000 men, half of whom were newly recruited black soldiers, poorly trained and equipped. The troops were camped in the open with just two gatling guns. They did not even have their wagons drawn into a circle, or laager, which local guides had advised them to do.

The British then split up their troops at Isandhlwana camp yet again by sending out scouting parties. One of these stumbled on the main Zulu army preparing to attack. They sent a messenger back to the camp. Instead of forming a tight square to fight from, the soldiers hastily took up defensive positions in a line in front of the hill.

At about 12.30, the Zulus attacked in their usual formation: a central group attacked head on, while two 'horns' of the army tried to circle round to the left and right to attack from behind. The British were well equipped to fight off the central attack. Those Zulus in the later waves of attack had to climb over the bodies of their dead comrades to reach the British. But they were brave and kept on going. Meanwhile, the 'horns' of the army had much better success. Because the British were strung out in a long line, they were relatively easy to get around. The 'horns' managed to break into the camp in just over an hour. Once inside, there was fierce hand-to-hand fighting with spears and bayonets. Finally, the British troops broke, overcome by the greater numbers of Zulus. They made off in various directions; mostly aiming for the Natal border. The Zulus broke up to chase them and finish them off; few escaped.

A total victory?

The Zulus won the battle of Isandhlwana, but it was not a straightforward victory. Almost as many Zulus as British died in the battle. The Zulus had taken on overconfident soldiers in a bad position and had won, but, even here, the better

The Battle of Isandhlwana.

weaponry of the British gave them an advantage. After Isandhlwana, the British took the Zulus far more seriously. In the fight that followed almost at once, at Rorke's Drift, the British fought from a tight defensive position of fortified buildings and won, even though greatly outnumbered. This reinforced the lesson of Isandhlwana. They should fight the Zulus in a defensive square or a laager of wagons, not strung out.

Another problem for the Zulus was that the British reaction to this defeat was not to make peace. Instead, they decided to crush the Zulus completely. From then on they waged 'total war'; taking no prisoners and burning Zulu settlements, crops and cattle as they went.

Work it out!

1 a What was the British commander's big mistake before Isandhlwana?

 b How might he have explained why he acted as he did?

2 a How was Isandhlwana a victory for the Zulus?

 b How was it less than a victory for the Zulus?

29

Advance on Ulundi

The British advanced on the Zulu capital of Ulundi. There were battles along the way. Both sides lost a lot of soldiers. However, the Zulus, who did not change their tactics greatly, lost more soldiers than the British. They kept on charging positions heavily defended with firearms. While they were undoubtedly brave in these attacks, there was little doubt as to the eventual outcome.

What happened after Ulundi?

The Zulu war did not have a tidy finish. There were no more big battles after Ulundi. It was clear that the British had won, but the Zulu tribal leaders and Cetshwayo did not sit down and sign a peace treaty. Cetshwayo fled north, hoping to raise a new army to attack the British again. Meanwhile, various tribal leaders decided to make peace with the British, rather than to rally to Cetshwayo. The British moved steadily north, making peace with tribal leaders along the way. Most of these leaders were hoping that, if they made peace, the British would let them run the country as an English colony.

Ulundi: the last battle

The Battle of Ulundi was not fought in Ulundi itself, but on the flat plain beyond it. Both sides thought this would be the decisive battle of the war. Both sides still wanted a big battle, on open ground.

On 4 July the British had crossed the river by daybreak, leaving behind a fortified laager. As soon as they were across the river they formed a square of soldiers and moved across the plain, slowly and awkwardly, in a square. They headed for a raised area with a good line of sight all round and little bush for cover for the Zulus. By 8.30 am both armies were in place; the British in their square and the Zulus in their usual 'two horn' formation. Wave after wave of Zulus attacked the square and tried to circle round and break in. They failed. Like Isandhlwana, the battle of Ulundi lasted about an hour, but this time it was the Zulus who retreated, pursued by the British. About 1,500 Zulus were killed at Ulundi, compared to about 30 British. Many of the Zulus were not killed in the battle itself, but in the long 'mopping up' operation that followed.

The surrender of Cetshwayo.

> *The Zulu war was a success for the British. They beat the Zulus and ended up owning Zululand.*

> *The Zulu war was a failure for the British. They even had to ask Cetshwayo to come back again. They lost lots and lots of soldiers.*

Work it out!

Which view do you agree with and why? Use the information on these pages to support your answer.

What happened to Cetshwayo?

Cetshwayo was eventually captured on 28 August. He surrendered to the British. Too many Zulu leaders had made peace with the British for him to try to hold out any longer. He was sent into exile in Cape Town, southern Africa. He was told he would not be allowed to return to Zululand. However, the British tried to put him back on the throne in 1883, hoping to stop the fighting between tribes that was tearing Zululand apart. It was unlikely that a king who had lost a war would be accepted back by a people that valued warrior skills highly. He failed to unite the country, and died in 1884, possibly from poison.

What happened to Zululand?

Cetshwayo's kingdom was broken up into thirteen kingdoms. This was, the British worked out, a large enough number to make it unlikely that they would all re-unite. The kingdom nearest to the Natal border was ruled by an Englishman, John Dunn. Other kingdoms were given to the tribal leaders who the British thought were most likely to stay loyal to Britain. The British were right, in that the thirteen leaders did not get on well enough to unite Zululand again. Indeed, they fought so often that the British even tried to re-instate Cetshwayo, to see if he could settle things down. This was a failure, and the British finally absorbed Zululand into the Union of South Africa.

What happened to Africa?

The British and other European countries continued to take over more and more of Africa to add to their empires. By 1914, over 95% of Africa had been colonised by European countries. It was not until the 1950s and 1960s that African countries began to regain their independence.

Cholera!

In autumn 1831 **cholera** hit Britain for the first time. It began in Sunderland and raged around the country until summer 1833. Because it was the first outbreak, we know less about it than later outbreaks. We cannot even be sure how many people died, as deaths did not have to be registered at this time. Some people did keep records. In 1848, when the second **epidemic** struck, Dr Thomas Shapter wrote a history of the 1832 cholera in Exeter, which he saw at first hand as a doctor in the local hospital.

SOURCE A

Summary of Privy Council list of cholera symptoms and possible treatment, 20 October 1831.

Symptoms

- giddiness, sickness, slow pulse, cramps in finger and toes, spreading to body
- vomiting, diarrhoea, inability to urinate
- skin colour darkens, eyes sink, fingers and toes seem to shrink and shrivel, nails have blue tinge
- skin is cold and damp, tongue is flabby, cold, with a white coating
- breathing and pulse irregular, patient finds it hard to breathe

Treatment

There is no known cure. A doctor should be sent for. The London Board of Health will send any new information to each Board of Health. It has been found to be helpful to:

- keep patient warm to keep circulation going – blankets on bed, poultices, bags of hot salt or bran
- wine, brandy or warming oils, such as oil of peppermint, should be drunk, if the patient can keep it down.

SOURCE B

Summary of Privy Council regulations to try to prevent cholera, 20 October 1831.

- Quarantine regulations in coast towns; local authorities to tell people that smugglers could carry cholera.
- Every town to set up a **Board of Health** – local magistrates, the vicar, three doctors (one to keep in touch with the Board of Health in London).
- Isolation is important. The Board must choose a place to isolate the sick, e.g. hospitals or barracks. If a family will not send their sick away, the whole house must be isolated and have a notice: 'sick'. When the sick person leaves, the house must be cleaned and the notice 'caution' put on the door. The rest of the family must be isolated until they are clear of the disease. A twenty-day period without sickness is advised; sickroom to be well ventilated. Food and other things to be left outside and collected when the streets are clear.
- To clean a house: remove all rubbish and burn it. Wash all clothes and furniture, etc. in boiling water. Wash walls and paintwork with hot water and lime. Sluice all drains and privies with hot water and chloride. Leave house empty and doors and windows open for at least a week. Those who die should be buried in special burial places.
- Places that have already had cholera report that it is most common among the poor, ill-fed and unhealthy and spreads most rapidly where streets are narrow, people crowded together and little attention is paid to cleanliness or ventilation.

SOURCE C

Cholera was a *contagious* disease. It could be spread by touch but also in polluted water. People did not know this in 1832. They did know that their drinking water (which mostly came from the rivers they pumped their sewage into) was dirty, as this cartoon from 1828 shows. But they did not realize that it could spread diseases like cholera.

SOURCE D

Another week has passed and London is still full of bitter and violent dispute over whether cholera has broken out there or not. This is despite the events in Sunderland, Gateshead and Musselburgh and the sad history in all parts of the world visited by cholera. In London it is still described by many as a 'humbug' and pretence made up to ruin trade with other countries.

From a medical journal published in 1832.

Work it out!

1 Draw an outline of a person. Mark on and colour in all the symptoms of cholera.

2 List some more ways to keep the patient warm – think carefully about whether the things you think of would have been available at the time.

3 a The London Board of Health had sent doctors to St Petersburg in Russia to study the cholera which was moving steadily across Europe. What two things did they feel were very important to help prevent the spread of cholera ?

   b What disease from an earlier period of history was treated in a similar way?

4 What kind of people do you think were trying to say that the cholera was just a made-up illness? Explain your answer.

Exeter in 1832

Exeter was a busy port in 1832. It was also a crowded city – the population had risen from about 18,000 in 1800 to about 28,000 in 1832. Dr Thomas Shapter came to Exeter in 1832, to work at the hospital during the cholera outbreak. His description of the city shows the problems of such rapid growth (see the box). Exeter set up a Board of Health (see Source B) as soon as the government suggested it. It was, after all, a busy port. Cholera struck on 19 July 1832. By 24 September, when the last case was reported, 402 people had died.

Sewage removal and water supply

The streets of the city are narrow with many **courts**, lanes and alleys leading off them. The paving, except in the main roads, is made of rounded pebbles, with the sides sloping down to the middle, which forms a gutter. This gutter is the only way of removing sewage and rubbish in most parts of the city. Some of the main roads, where the wealthier people live, have recently had sewers built, but most of the city has not. The water supply of the city is not sufficient for the needs of the people there. People fetch their own water from the river and nearby streams, or buy it from water carriers.

Dirt and overcrowding

The reports of the District committees speak of houses occupied by up to fifteen families, huddled together in dirty rooms; of slaughter houses in Butchers Row surrounded by rotting heaps of **offal**; of pigs and poultry kept in sheds and cellars; of sewage heaps everywhere.

Dr Thomas Shapter's description.

SOURCE E

Burning tar in barrels in Butchers Row during the cholera epidemic.

The Board's first recommendations

- The city must employ more people to clean the streets and courts, especially in the poorer parts of the city.
- Pumps and wells must be cleaned and repaired and new wells must be started.
- The **Corporation of the Poor** (who collected money for looking after Exeter's poor) must remind the poor to keep clean. They should consider employing poor people to clean and whitewash homes in the poorer areas, before cholera strikes.
- Notices must be put up stressing the need to keep clean and ventilate houses. The symptoms of cholera must be given, with details of what to do if it strikes.
- A place for the sick, and people to care for them, must be chosen.
- To pay for all this, the Board will ask the wealthier residents of the city for voluntary contributions to add to money raised by the Corporation of the Poor.

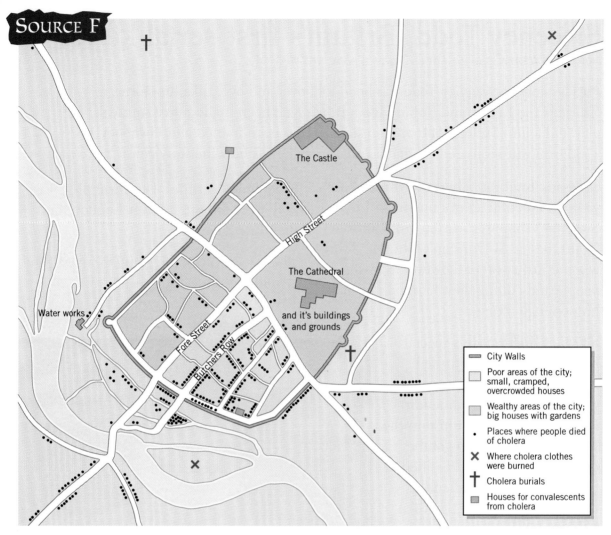

A copy of Dr Shapter's map showing where deaths from cholera occurred in 1832.

Map legend:
- City Walls
- Poor areas of the city; small, cramped, overcrowded houses
- Wealthy areas of the city; big houses with gardens
- Places where people died of cholera
- X Where cholera clothes were burned
- † Cholera burials
- Houses for convalescents from cholera

Map labels: The Castle, High Street, The Cathedral and it's buildings and grounds, Water works, Fore Street, Butchers Row

Problems with money

Different cities had different rules about raising money for the poor. The Exeter system allowed people to choose whether or not to give money. The Corporation of the Poor did not raise much extra money. The Board's appeals for voluntary contributions did not raise much, either. So when the cholera finally broke out, the Board had not been able to find a building in which to isolate the sick, or a suitable burial ground for the dead, let alone whitewash the homes of the poor in advance. Eventually, the Board had to make people pay a set amount.

Work it out!

1 a What parts of Exeter were seen as the most likely to suffer an outbreak of cholera?

 b Referring to the information about conditions in Exeter, can you name any streets in particular that were likely to be hit by cholera?

 c Were any precautions taken there?

 d From looking at the map of outbreaks of cholera, did the precautions work?

2 a Why were the sensible 'clean-up' suggestions suggested by the Board of Health not done before the cholera hit?

 b Why might people act like this?

Sweeney Todd, Britain's first serial killer?

The story of Sweeney Todd has been told over and over, like the stories of Jack the Ripper and Robin Hood. It has even been made into a musical play and a film. At least one pizza restaurant has been named after Sweeney Todd; you will soon see why that is gruesome. This is how the story goes:

Sweeney Todd was a **barber**, who had a shop off Fleet Street in London in 1785. Sweeney's shop was in Hen and Chicken Court, beside St Dunstan's Church. Todd was not just a barber, however. Shaving people and cutting their hair did not make him enough money.

Sweeney Todd made a special barber's chair, which turned upside down. When someone who looked well off came into the shop, Sweeney sat him in the special chair. He then got the customer ready to shave, lifted his chin carefully, and cut his throat from ear to ear! He then pulled a hidden lever. The chair flipped over on a floorboard, which had an identical chair on the other side. Almost immediately, everything was back to normal.

When Todd next had a free moment he went down to the cellar, stripped the corpse of all its possessions and handed it over to Mrs Lovett, his accomplice. Mrs Lovett ran a pie shop in Bell Yard, just around the corner from Todd's barber shop. Some versions of the story say he took the corpses from his shop to hers along a secret tunnel between the two. Mrs Lovett then proceeded to cook the evidence of Sweeney's crimes. Her meat pies, it is said, were famous all over London for their fine flavour… .

The question you are going to investigate is 'Did Sweeney Todd really exist?'

SOURCE A

Denis Quilley, the actor, in a theatrical performance of Sweeney Todd.

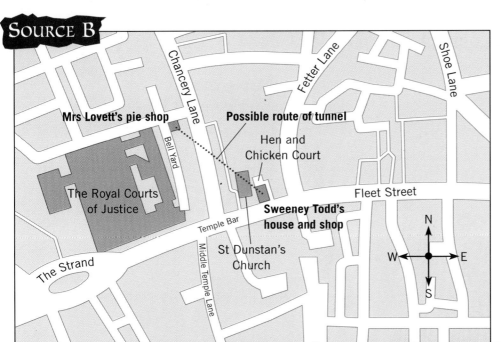

Map of Fleet Street and Hen and Chicken Court, as described in the Sweeney Todd story.

The Royal Courts of Justice

Mrs Lovett's pie shop

Bell Yard

Chancery Lane

Possible route of tunnel

Fetter Lane

Shoe Lane

Hen and Chicken Court

Fleet Street

Sweeney Todd's house and shop

Temple Bar

St Dunstan's Church

The Strand

Middle Temple Lane

N
W ● E
S

Fleet Street, looking west, painted by George Scharf in August 1830.

SOURCE C

SOURCE D

A horrid murder has been committed in Fleet Street on the person of a young gentleman from the country on a visit to his relatives in London. While walking through the city, he chanced to stop to admire the striking clock of St Dunstan's Church, and there fell into conversation with a man dressed as a barber. The two men began to argue. Suddenly the barber took from his clothing a razor and slit the throat of the young man, thereafter disappearing into the alleyway of Hen and Chicken Court, and was seen no more.

From *The Annual Register*, a London newspaper, April 1785.

Work it out!

1 Does Source C support the map of the location of Sweeney Todd's crimes?

2 a What elements of the Sweeney Todd story does Source D support?

   b What elements of the Sweeney Todd story does Source D not support?

   c Are there any elements of the Sweeney Todd story that Source D actually contradicts?

37

Digging deeper into the Todd mystery

An illustration from *Sweeney Todd, The Demon Barber of Fleet Street*, written in 1878.

SOURCE F

I instituted a careful search of the vaults beneath St Dunstan's Church, and I found a secret passage to the cellar of the pie shop in Bell Yard. I later found a similar passage to the cellar under Sweeney Todd's shop. Upon reaching this cellar, the first thing I saw was a chair fixed to the roof by its legs. The plank on which this chair rested turned upon its centre, and could be made to turn by a simple contrivance above, so that any unfortunate person could be let down in a moment, and the vacant chair would come up and take the place of the one that had been above.

From *Sweeney Todd, The Demon Barber of Fleet Street*, an extended version of the Sweeney Todd story, written in 1878.

SOURCE G

When I was a young Londoner I was shown in Fleet Street the very shop of the Demon Barber – and shuddered to think that meat pies were still on sale there.

From *Playgoer's Memories*, written by H.G. Hibbert in 1920.

SOURCE H

I did some research in the old street directories [these directories list street names, numbers and occupants for each year]. Despite an exhaustive search through the directories of London through the years 1768 to 1850, I could find no Sweeney Todd.

Said by the historian N.G. Lofts, quoted in *Sweeney Todd*, a historian's investigation of the story, written in 1979.

SOURCE I

Towards the end of the fourteenth century
There lived a sort of demon barber,
Who slit his clients' throats at 24 Rue des
  Marmouzets.

He carried on this horrible trade
And nobody could resist him,
In his cellar he polished them off,
His accomplice a villainous Pie Merchant
  next door.

This horrid tale also tells us
That he worked with a ferocious female
Fiercer than the fiercest bailiff.
For all the poor devils he killed
His partner converted into pork pies
And they said of his customers when dead,
They are gone – pork creatures.

An English translation of a French song, sung from about 1450 onwards.

It could be made up. But it fits the map – it was made up about a real place, I suppose. There <u>was</u> a barber who killed someone there too.

The story is made up. People just like that gory stuff. So they made it up around a song they remembered or a fairy tale. Look at the map – the pies being eaten by all those judges is too good to miss!

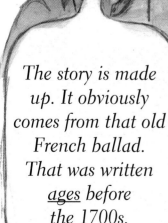

The story is made up. It obviously comes from that old French ballad. That was written <u>ages</u> before the 1700s.

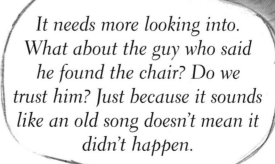

It needs more looking into. What about the guy who said he found the chair? Do we trust him? Just because it sounds like an old song doesn't mean it didn't happen.

Work it out!

Which view do you agree with and why? Use as many of the sources as possible to back up your answer.

Football rules!

People have played football since medieval times. Early football was a wild game, with no set rules. People played on varying sizes of pitch (even from village to village across the fields) and various sizes and shapes of ball. Every time two teams met to play they had to begin by deciding what rules to play by. Injuries were common. In Victorian times football became organized. Rules were drawn up. Football became a sport to watch, not just a game to play on odd holidays. How and why did this happen?

The Football Association (FA) was set up in 1863 in London *'for the purpose of forming an Association to lay down a definite code of rules for the game'*. The rules were published on 1 December 1863. They were adapted from rules used at Uppingham public school. Everyone who joined the FA had to play by these rules. Soon clubs were playing each other countrywide. The FA Cup and a yearly England v Scotland match were set up. Teams began to practice regularly, to wear a 'uniform' and to set up their own grounds. Matches drew in bigger crowds. Football began to attract players and spectators from all classes, increasingly from the working class.

The FA believed in keeping football an amateur game. They agreed that players who had jobs should be paid for 'wages lost' while playing, but they did not believe in professional, paid teams. However, this ignored the fact that players had to get their employers' permission to take time off to play and practise. The problem was especially severe in northern industrial towns, where a passion for football had developed. Here, clubs used the 'wages lost' rule to employ players full time – to field a professional team, in fact. The FA ignored the problem. It grew. In 1883 there were so many allegations of 'professionalism' in industrial towns like Blackburn, Sheffield and Birmingham that the FA was forced to hold an inquiry into the matter.

SOURCE A

The first rules:

1 It is a goal if a ball is kicked or headed through the posts and under the bar.
2 Hands can be used only to stop a ball and put it by the handler's feet.
3 Kicks must be aimed at the ball.
4 The ball cannot be kicked in the air.
5 No tripping or heel kicking.
6 If a ball is kicked off the side of the pitch, the player who kicked it out must kick it back in, towards the centre, from the spot where it crossed the line.
7 If a ball is kicked over the goal line, a player from the side whose goal it is shall kick it back on to the pitch.
8 No player may stand within six paces of a player kicking the ball back into play.
9 Players must keep behind the ball.
10 No player can be charged once the ball is behind him.

Going to the match?

From 1854 onwards the government reduced working hours and, in some cases, fixed wages. More and more firms began to give employees Saturday afternoon off as well. Many working people now had more leisure time and some money to spend once the weekly bills were paid. In many industrial towns people were within walking distance of their local football ground. Even if they were not, it was now possible for people to travel more easily. Rail travel was cheap, especially on excursion trains. Cheap tram and bus fares encouraged people to travel further and faster too.

An engraving from the *Illustrated Sporting and Dramatic News* of 20 February 1875. It shows football players practising dribbling.

In 1884, the manager of Preston North End admitted that he and many northern clubs paid their players. By July 1885 the FA had been forced to accept professional players. But there was still a lot of bad feeling between professional and amateur sides, so in 1888, some of the biggest professional teams broke away to form the Football League. They were: Everton, Notts County, Stoke, Preston North End, Burnley, Wolverhampton, Aston Villa, Blackburn Rovers, Accrington, West Bromwich, Derby County.

What price skill?

In 1881 a player for Blackburn Rovers, Suter, was paid £100 'for his services' to stop him playing for local rivals, Darwen, instead. It is unclear whether this was an extra payment, on top of the wages that Blackburn were already openly paying to players, but it was a very large sum. At the time, the average textile worker earned about £60 a year.

Work it out!

1 a Why do you think there were so many rules and variations in early football?

  b What changes in the Victorian period made organizing the game on a countrywide scale more possible and desirable?

2 a Why do you think the FA thought that football should remain an amateur game?

  b How did they make provision for working people being part of a team?

  c How did this fail to take account of the actual circumstances of working people?

3 Why do you think there were still disputes in the FA, even once they had accepted professional players?

From roads to railways: transport 1750-1900

In 1750 methods of transport had changed little since medieval times. Most people travelled by foot, on horseback, by wagon or carriage, or by boat. Whatever method you chose, it was very slow. The process of industrialisation was just beginning and there was a growing need for better methods of transport to bring supplies to the factories and to take the finished goods to new and increasingly distant markets.

Some famous engineers			
Name	**Previous occupation**	**Dates**	**Length of roads built**
George Wade	Soldier	1673–1748	400km
John Metcalf	Smuggler	1717–1810	288km
John Macadam	Businessman	1756–1836	1600km
Thomas Telford	Stonemason	1757–1834	1600km

Roads – the turnpike trusts

Most roads had a bad reputation. One eighteenth century traveller, Arthur Young, wrote to 'warn all travellers who may decide to travel through this terrible northern country to avoid it as they would the devil!' His comments, whilst not untypical, do not give the whole truth. Some roads were being improved and were becoming a pleasure to travel on. These were the turnpike trusts. An **entrepreneur** would raise some money and use it to build a high quality road. He would then charge people to use the road. At the end of each stretch of road there would be gates (called the turnpike) and a tollhouse where travellers were stopped and asked to pay their **toll**. Different tolls would be charged to different travellers. A horseman would be charged much less than a wagon laden with goods for market. Daniel Defoe wrote in 1724 that 'the benefit of a good road more than makes up for the small charge the travellers have to pay at the turnpikes.'

Not everyone agreed with Defoe. There were riots on some stretches of road, and turnpikes and tollhouses were set on fire by crowds angry at being charged to travel on the roads. Many felt that these roads should be free for everyone. However, as time went on, most people saw that these improved roads brought great benefits. More traffic on the roads created more work for people such as road builders, coach builders, innkeepers, and grooms. Trade increased and there was a wider choice of goods for the public. This increase in trade also led to a fall in prices at market, and an increase in jobs. This had an obvious benefit for everyone.

The road builders

Who built these roads? There were no government regulations regarding road building. Anyone who could raise the money and obtain the consent of Parliament could build what he liked. This meant that roads differed greatly in their construction and condition. The owner of the road might have used

A painting of a Royal Mail coach on the road near Kew Bridge in 1835. Notice the toll gate on the bridge.

poor-quality materials so that he could make more profit. Repairs might be delayed or even not done at all. However, this was not the case with the majority of the roads, and engineers began to make great advances in road building.

Improved roads helped to create a 'Golden Age of Coaching' in the 1820s and 1830s. Travellers could now expect to travel in relative comfort and with reasonable speed. A journey from London to Edinburgh took ten days in 1750; in 1830 it took just two. The fastest coaches were the mail coaches. These were a tremendous sight and sound, with their bright yellow and black colours and the coachman blowing his horn to warn the tollhouse-keeper to open the gates. The mail coach took precedence over all other traffic and did not have to pay tolls at the turnpikes.

Yet the 'Golden Age' soon ended. The development of the canal network for carrying goods and then the coming of the railways meant that by the 1830s there was safer, faster and cheaper travel by train. The long-distance coaches disappeared.

Canals

The poor state of the roads meant that rivers were used to transport heavy or bulky goods. But rivers can flood, or catch boats on sandbanks. Rivers do not always go in the right direction either. The answer was canals – man-made rivers to just the right width and depth and going in the right direction.

The Duke of Bridgewater employed James Brindley to build him a canal from his coal mine outside Manchester into the city.

By July 1761 boats were regularly taking coal to Manchester at 2p per cart. It had cost 8p a horse load before the canal was cut. Local factories bought the coal in huge quantities. The workers in Manchester could buy cheaper coal for their fires. The Duke became a very rich man and others who wanted to try to copy his success followed his lead.

Josiah Wedgwood, for instance, the pottery manufacturer, invested £1000 in the planned Grand Trunk Canal. This was a massive scheme to link the rivers Trent and Severn. It took Brindley eleven years to build the canal. Eventually, canals connected most of the main cities and

43

rivers. During the 1790s there was 'canal mania' and many smaller canals were built which did not make a profit. Canals connecting the main industrial centres were profitable, and by the early 1800s some canals boats were beginning to take passengers. However, the canals could not compete with the railways.

The first railways

The first railways were wagon ways taking coal from the pits to the river. As the coal was very heavy, the wagons moved more easily on rails. These rails were at first made of wood and then, later, iron-plated or iron rails were used. Initially horses pulled the wagons. These were later replaced by stationary steam engines which pulled the wagons along on ropes. It was not long before a mining engineer thought of putting wheels on the engine and letting it pull the wagon on the rails. The engineer was Richard Trevithick, though he never developed his idea beyond a kind of fairground attraction.

Another engineer, George Stephenson was interested in steam engines. He built sixteen whilst working at Killingworth Mine, near Newcastle upon Tyne. Stephenson met a group of businessmen who had just received permission, through an Act of Parliament, to build a railway from Stockton to Darlington. The original idea had been to pull the wagons by horse. Stephenson suggested using a locomotive engine.

The businessmen agreed, and in 1825 the first commercial railway was opened. It was a great success. Soon Stephenson was appointed by another group of businessmen to build a railway from Liverpool to Manchester. When the line was built a competition was held (the Rainhill Trials) to see whose engine would operate on the line. Stephenson's own design, named 'The Rocket', won.

In 1830, the first passenger railway was opened. It took no time at all for railways to spread out across Britain.

In 1830 there were just 50 miles of track; by 1850 this had risen to 6,084 miles of track and to 21,429 miles of track in 1897.

The canals of England in the early nineteenth century. The 'Grand Cross' canals linked the four major English rivers: the Thames, the Severn, the Mersey and the Trent. This meant that goods could be transported by canal to any of the main English ports.

The steam locomotive 'Catch me who can' built by Richard Trevithick and seen in Euston Square in London in 1809.

Railways were carrying over a million passengers. Just as in the story of the development of turnpikes and canals, there was a period of 'railway mania' in the 1840s, as investors saw a way to make a quick profit. Again a few made a lot of money but most lost their investment. Despite this, railways were to remain the main form of travel until well into the twentieth century.

The influence of the railways

Railways had a great effect on British industry. They created a great number of employment opportunities. Drivers were needed to drive the trains; engineers needed to build the trains and railtrack. Both the iron and coal industries did very well out of supplying the railway industry. A wide network of stations had to be built and staffed.

Railways also had a great effect on society in general. People could now expect fresh food and fish to be delivered; a journey of two days by road would take less than ten hours by train. People could go to the seaside on holiday and they could **commute** to work rather than live in the filthy towns. Railways made the nation more uniform. National newspapers could be produced because everyone could read them on the same day. As many goods became available across the country national advertising began. It also meant that the post became quicker and cheaper.

First, second and third class travel on the Manchester to Liverpool railway.

Work it out!

1 How did the setting up of turnpike trusts improve the roads in the eighteenth century? Were all turnpike roads an improvement?

2 Why were canals such a good method of transport for industrialists such as Josiah Wedgwood?

3 Design a poster advertising the Rainhill Trials. It can either be aimed at engineers to produce a steam engine for the competition or at attracting an audience to the competition.

4 What arguments could you use to say that railways helped to unite the people of Great Britain? Read your answers over again. Do you think that railways were important in uniting the people of Great Britain? Give reasons for your answer.

Slum-living in Victorian times

At the beginning of the nineteenth century most people lived in the country. Although their living conditions were not luxurious, they were usually in their own cottages with access to adequate supplies of water. By the middle of the century, many people were living in the newly industrialised towns. These people had arrived in such numbers that there were not enough houses, and new houses were thrown up as quickly and cheaply as possible. Houses were overcrowded and had very poor **sanitation**. They became breeding grounds for very **contagious** and dangerous diseases. So what was it like to live in one of these towns?

Many towns grew rapidly as men and women arrived to find work in the new factories. In 1744 Glasgow had a population of just 24,000. A visitor in 1760 called it 'one of the prettiest towns in all of Europe.' By 1856 the population had risen to just under 400,000. An observer in 1850 described Glasgow as 'possibly the filthiest and unhealthiest of all the towns of Britain'. Contemporary descriptions of the industrial towns often spoke of black smoke that was 'veiling the sun' or 'covering the sky'. A description of South Shields near Newcastle in 1851 describes it as: 'Generally enveloped by a dense atmosphere of smoke, from the coal pit, glassworks and other manufactories.'

Working-class houses

Unfortunately there were no laws controlling the conditions the workers lived in. Overcrowding was made worse by the fact that there was no cheap public transport. People had to be near to their place of work. Many landlords saw an opportunity for quick and easy profit. Terraces of back-to-back houses were built to house the poor, crammed in beside the railways.

The 1861 **census** of South Shields gives details of one room up and one room down houses in Cornwallis Square. Number five had twenty-two people living in it, and number eleven had five separate families and a lodger!

The worst houses were in the **courts**. These were enclosed passageways with buildings all around. There was little sunlight, the ground was often blocked with rubbish and sewage, the cellars, where families lived, were often full of water. Sometimes there was only one water tap and one toilet for the whole court, either a cesspit which could leak into the water system, or a system of buckets that would be collected at night. In Liverpool, 55,535 people lived in 1,982 courts.

SOURCE A

'the inhabitants are generally remarkably sober, industrious and orderly; but are in much need of improved ideas as to domestic cleanliness and comfort…

Buildings in this town which are always badly ventilated and almost always destitute of necessary conveniences, have led to the formation of habits among the poorer classes, which are not only disgusting and unwholesome, but which are quite inconsistent with a high tone of morals.'

Comment on housing in South Shields, near Newcastle upon Tyne in north-east England.

The growth of Leeds

The town of Leeds seen in a drawing of 1715 in Source B seems to have changed little from a description written nearly a hundred years before: 'An ancient market town standing in a fruitful valley on the north side of the river... a broad, paved street leads north from the stone bridge'.

In the view of 1858 (Source C), the factory chimneys, the railway and the rows of workmen's cottages are clearly seen. Leeds had long been a centre for the wool trade: with the coming of new machines and the canals and railways, the town grew rapidly and so did the export of wool and cloth. The population trebled between 1801 and 1851, from 53,000 to 172,000. A local journal of 1843 wrote: 'the lower parts of the town next to the river are dirty and crowded...owing to a general lack of draining and an abundance of courts and blind alleys'.

SOURCE C

Disease!

An increase in horse-drawn traffic, such as the hansom cabs, filled the roads with manure which attracted huge numbers of flies. With the flies came disease. Packing people so tightly together also helped to spread disease.

Contagious diseases such as typhoid, dysentery and cholera spread very fast and could be killers. Diarrhoea, when there was no regular supply of fresh, clean water, could also be a killer, especially for the old and young. These diseases spread as a direct result of the dirt and rubbish. Overcrowding helped cause further diseases such as tuberculosis, scarlet fever, whooping cough, diphtheria and measles. Unfortunately for the population, the medical authorities did not really understand what caused these diseases.

narrow court

enclosed on all four sides apart from the alleyway at the entrance

back-to-back houses (i.e. another court on the other side)

entrance through tunnel

communal toilet

no kitchens

cellars

water standpipe

open sewer or gutter

Drawing to show the plan of a Victorian court.

'Leave well alone!'

The Government was reluctant to get involved with the problems of the poor. This was because there were too many **vested interests** keen to keep the **status quo**. Many people did not like the idea of the Government becoming involved in the everyday lives of the citizens. They believed that a person's private life was his own business. The problem for the poor was that really they had no choice in where they lived, especially if they wished to work. The people who owned the houses did not wish to pay out huge sums of money to provide adequate piped water. The companies who supplied the standing taps did not wish to lose this profitable business. Finally, the people who would have to pay for any changes to the sewage system would be the rich and they were not keen to pay higher taxes for something that would not benefit them directly. What was to change many middle-class minds was the fact that the infectious diseases knew no class barriers. Even Prince Albert, Queen Victoria's husband, was to die of typhoid in 1861.

The campaign to improve public health

Edwin Chadwick led a campaign to try and improve the health of the people. In his *Report on the Sanitary Conditions of the Labouring Population of Great Britain* (1842) he blamed dirt, not poverty, as the overriding factor; and he blamed the authorities not the people themselves as being at fault.

By the end of the nineteenth century housing conditions were still poor for many people, but at least efforts were being made to improve them. Local authorities could build their own homes to replace insanitary ones, though it was not until the twentieth century that it became normal to have adequate water and sewage pipes in virtually every home.

Chadwick's report

In his report Edwin Chadwick found four main causes for the spread of disease:
- Filth
- Damp
- Overcrowding
- Lack of pure water

He recommended four solutions:
- Cleaner streets
- Better drainage
- Better ventilation
- Better water supply

The first Public Health Act of 1848 was not effective because it allowed councils to address the problems only if they wanted to. They were not forced to do anything unless the death rate went above twenty-three in every thousand people.

A second act, the Public Health Act of 1875, was much more specific. All local authorities had to appoint a Medical Officer; they had to be responsible for refuse collection, main sewers and fresh water supply. More importantly, all new homes had to have piped water and adequate sanitation.

Work it out!

1 Write a paragraph about each of the following causes of poor living conditions in towns:

   a Industry

   b Overcrowding

   c Inadequate water/sewage supplies

   d Poor housing

   e Government policies.

2 In your opinion, which of the five causes in question 1 was the main cause of the poor living conditions? Explain why you have made the choice you have.

3 People were aware of the living conditions to be found in the towns. Why do you think that they were still willing to go and live in the towns?

4 Draw a cartoon, highlighting one, or more, of the dangerous living conditions discussed in this chapter. Remember the point of the cartoon is to emphasise to your readers that something must be done to improve the situation.

'We are amused': entertainment in the Victorian age

One image which many people have of the Victorian period is of a time of hardship and **drudgery** for the working classes, with work, particularly in the factories, taking up every waking hour and leaving no time for leisure. Another common image is that of Queen Victoria dressed in black, mourning the death of her husband, and stating severely that 'We are not amused!' There is some truth behind these images, but the people of the Victorian times also knew how to enjoy themselves.

At the beginning of the nineteenth century, most entertainment took place on Sundays and on political and church holidays such as Christmas Day, Shrove Tuesday or Guy Fawkes Day. As most people lived in the country, the village inn was the centre of any organised activity, and villagers played games such as football, skittles, quoits, wrestling and prize fighting. These would have been subject to much gambling, as were other less civilised activities such as badger or bear baiting, cock-fighting and bull-running.

Major sporting events in the region, especially horse racing, attracted people from all classes. Although the inter-village football matches could lead to violent and riotous behaviour, there was no trouble when large crowds assembled at Kersal Moor to watch the Manchester races just days after the **Peterloo** massacre. Workers would also take days off to see the ever-popular public executions and to hear speakers at election time, even though they could not vote.

More factories – less leisure?

It has been thought that the growth of industry meant that there was less time for leisure for the working classes. This was not really the case. It was not until the late 1800s that the majority of workers were employed in factories. Most workers were still farm labourers. Secondly, not all workers worked all day every day. **Hewers** in the north-east coal-fields worked a seven-hour shift, and others, such as dockers, were casual labour, working only when needed. Finally, factory owners were not always in such complete control as is so readily assumed. Many workers had a habit of taking 'Saint Monday' off work, as and when they wanted, and when they could afford to. The factory owners did not like this but so many workers did it they had to let it pass. As a direct result of this practice, the 1850 Factory Act was passed, giving textile workers the Saturday afternoon off, as well as all day Sunday. This ended the tendency to take 'Saint Monday' off. Not surprisingly, most other factories soon followed suit, without the need for legislation.

Trains to the sea!

It was the invention of the railway that was to change the way the working classes spent their leisure time. Railways gradually opened up the possibility of travel for all. Working-class families could take day trips, especially to the seaside. A coach from London to Brighton in 1830 would cost £1.20 and take five hours. A train in 1840 cost 40p and took just over two hours. (But 40p was still nearly half the average weekly wage of a textile worker.) Seaside resorts sprang up all along the

Paddington station, painted by William Frith in 1862.

coast. Southend, Cleethorpes and Blackpool were popular among the working class, while the middle classes patronised Brighton or Scarborough. Thomas Cook organised a cheap day out for 500 **temperance** workers from Leicester to Loughborough. It was a great success. Cook then set about organising trips to see the Great Exhibition in London. Thousands of working-class people went to see the Exhibition. (They are the reason that public conveniences were built in London, as many feared widespread indecent exposures otherwise!) The practice of going on day trips was further helped by the introduction of Bank Holidays in 1871.

Organising football

The working men who moved from the villages into the new industrial towns took their love of football with them. The formation of teams was encouraged by factory managers and also religious enthusiasts and moralists hoping to keep young men out of trouble. Teams like Everton, Southampton and Aston Villa were started this way. Teams were also started by groups of workers. Arsenal was made up of munitions workers; workers who got Wednesday afternoon off set up Sheffield Wednesday. In 1863, The Football Association was set up and the FA Cup was instigated. In the 1883 Cup Final the working-class Blackburn Olympic beat the upper-class Old Etonians and football became the working man's game. Cheap rail travel meant that supporters could travel to watch their team play. Professionalism meant that working-class men could play football as a job.

And many other pastimes...

Not all workers played football. Many men fished, or kept racing pigeons. From the 1830s onwards, allotments became popular in the built-up areas of railways and towns. Miners and railwaymen were considered the best gardeners. Some factory owners provided brass instruments, or pipes and drums in Scotland, for their workers to play in bands, and this to some extent helped to form the **Salvation Army**. Some men were members of the Armed Forces reserves. Often these pursuits excluded women, but two areas where

The 1883 FA Cup Final.

women were not excluded were the pubs and the Music Halls. Pubs did allow women, and many of them saw the pub as their only chance of relaxation away from the trials at home. Pubs were the province of the working classes, and despite all efforts to close them down, they survived and grew in importance over the century. Music Halls provided a range of entertainers, from acrobats and singers to dancers and actors, also for the working classes; the middle classes would go to the theatre to see a play or hear a recital.

Middle-class women at leisure – or was it good works?

The nature of middle-class leisure was that it should 'enhance the mind'. Often it was the influence of **evangelical** religion that directed what women did with their time.

Women involved themselves in **temperance** groups, prison reform, and the prevention of cruelty to children and animals. Their social life revolved around the church, with its bazaars, teas, Sunday Schools and choirs. Most middle-class women had servants and were more likely than men to have time to devote to these interests and good works. Clergymen were quick to tap into this source of willing labour.

Observers of the middle class stressed the importance of the home as a place for leisure. Middle-class women would play the piano and sing. They would read, especially aloud, the novels by Dickens or Trollope. They would embroider, as 'hands should never be idle'. However true this picture is, it is not the whole picture. Provincial theatres suffered a decline in the early 1800s, but the new middle classes

53

enjoyed going to the theatre and this decline soon turned around.

Thomas Cook, after his success with trips to the Great Exhibition, set his sights abroad. He arranged trips to see the International Exhibition in Paris in 1855. He then went on to organise trips to France, Switzerland and Italy. By the 1890s, Cook's son, John, was even arranging trips to see the pyramids in Egypt. This outraged the upper classes, who had always seen foreign travel as their preserve. Amongst the intellectual and professional classes, mountaineering was becoming popular. Even the last preserve of the upper classes, the hunt, was now being taken up by the wealthy factory owners.

It can be seen that the Victorians did know how to enjoy themselves. What is evident though is that leisure activities were as much part of the class system as the rest of society. There were rules and codes that must be followed. The one really classless game was cricket; it was played and watched by everyone. In this sense it can truly be called the national sport.

SOURCE C

The Penny Reading was a form of entertainment that was still going strong in the 'nineties. For it the schoolroom was lent, free of charge, and the pennies taken at the door paid for heating and light. It was a popular as well as an inexpensive entertainment. Everybody went; whole families together, and all agreed that the excitement of going out after dark, carrying lanterns, and sitting in a warm room with rows and rows of other people, was well worth the sum of one penny, apart from the entertainment provided.

The star turn was given by an old gentleman who, in his youth, had heard Dickens read his own works in public. He aimed to copy the great writer, and he drew tears from the women and throat-clearings from the men with his renderings of deathbed scenes and Oliver Twist asking for more. His audience loved to listen, for they were not readers, and they were waiting, a public ready-made, for the coming of the wireless and the cinema.

An extract from a story of country life at the end of the nineteenth century, written by Flora Thompson.

Work it out!

1 a List the different sports and leisure activities followed by the Victorians.

   b From the list, which sports and leisure activities are not followed today?

   c Which sports and leisure activities do you enjoy that are not on the list?

2 Explain how travel developed as a leisure activity over the period. You must include the key words/phrases: railways, Thomas Cook, 1850 Factory Act, the Great Exhibition, Bank Holidays, football.

3 Why do you think that there are very few leisure activities pursued by women in this chapter? Give as many reasons as you can, trying not to say simply that men were 'sexist'!

4 Write a newspaper article describing the FA Cup Final match of 1883 and its possible importance.

Factory reform for women and children

Throughout history women and children have played a major part in working life. Yet in the nineteenth century steps were taken to change the way that they were treated. Limitations were placed on the employment of women, and laws passed to try to prevent children from working for money altogether.

Why employ women and children in the new factories?

When the new factories began to appear, owners were keen to employ women and children as workers. Why? The main reason was that they were cheaper than men to employ and they were easier to control, as they were more likely to accept the harsh conditions. A further factor was the fact that the machines in the new factories used water, and later steam, power. This meant that physical strength was less important. Employers wanted workers who could crawl under machines to recover fallen material or who had neat hands and fingers to work machinery efficiently. Many women and children had these skills.

Harsh conditions

Because the factories were new, they did not have any regulations or laws to control them. They had no traditions nor accepted routines. They were noisy, hot and overcrowded. Workers had to accept the harsh and often contradictory system of fines, whereby they were fined up to a third of their week's wages for being dirty or for being caught washing themselves.

They worked very long hours. It was very easy to find examples of children as young as six working fourteen hours a day. They might start at five or six in the morning and not finish until seven in the evening. Very little time would be set aside for breaks. In a very busy period workers would start at three in the morning and work until ten at night.

It was not just the hours that were long. Workers could be brutally treated (see Source A).

SOURCE A

The men and big lads beat me with their hands many times, perhaps once or twice a week. This makes me cry. They beat me if I break a plate.

A comment from an eleven-year-old child who worked in the pottery industry in the north of England.

Workers, too, were always in danger of serious accidents. The machines did not have any guards to protect the women and children from getting caught. It was not uncommon for workers to lose limbs this way.

Wages were not good and varied widely from factory to factory. In Richard Arkwright's mill at Cromford the average wage was 3s 6d ($17\frac{1}{2}$ pence). A child might earn 1s 6d ($7\frac{1}{2}$ pence) a week, if he or she earned anything. It was common practice for a factory owner to look after pauper children. These children would be taken from the Poor Law Authorities. In return for their feeding, clothing and bed they would be expected to work in the factories without being paid.

An engraving of 1840 showing child workers in a mill being punished.

Later, factory owners paid their workers using a 'truck' system. What this meant was that workers would have part of their wages paid in tokens, rather than cash. These tokens could be spent only in the factory shop, where the price of goods was high and the quality low.

Why did opposition to women and children working in factories grow?

When the family had all worked on the land, everyone had a job to do. In the **domestic system**, again, everyone had a set job. The men wove, the women spun, the old women carded and the children did the chores. When the new mills opened it seemed natural that women and children who had come from the country would work in them. From the mid-1830s, 50 per cent of workers in the mills were women (about 125,000), and a further 13 per cent were children under the age of fourteen (about 31,000).

Reformers

Some people did want to change and improve working conditions in factories. These factory reformers felt that women working in mills had a negative effect on the family. By working some people felt these women became bad housewives and mothers. Working women were blamed for making their husbands go to the pub. The argument went that if the women went to work, they would not make a house homely, so the man would not want to stay in the home, but go to the pub instead. It is interesting to note that when Lord Shaftesbury led the campaign to end women working in the factories, he did not lead a similar campaign to end women working as servants. This was considered suitable work for women, and was acceptable.

Shaftesbury was not the only reformer. Richard Oastler led the Ten-Hour Movement (trying to limit the working day to ten hours). Other reformers pointed out that, for black people, slavery had been abolished but it still existed for pauper children.

Better conditions

Not all the factory owners were cruel and harsh, however. The best example of a 'good' factory owner is Robert Owen. Owen was considered unusual in the early part of the nineteenth century because he educated his workers' children, and did not employ them in his factory until they were at least nine. Owen also provided his workers with decent houses, refused to operate a 'truck' shop, and sold basic foodstuffs and household items at cost price. Owen did this in part because he had a social conscience, yet he also knew that if he treated his workers with respect they would work harder for him and he would make more profit. Which is exactly what happened.

The factory owner, Robert Owen.

SOURCE D

Reforms

Unfortunately, few factory owners copied Robert Owen. The main reforms to working conditions had to come from the laws passed by Parliament. The table on page 58 shows the main Acts passed in the nineteenth century.

	Factory Acts
1819	Children under nine not allowed to work *Not enforced due to a lack of inspectors*
1833	Children under nine not allowed to work Children aged between nine and thirteen limited to a nine-hour day
1844	Women limited to twelve hours work a day
1847	Women limited to ten hours work a day (textiles)
1867	Women limited to ten hours work a day
1874	Children under nine not allowed to work in textile factories
1878	Children under ten not allowed to work in factories
1901	Children under twelve not allowed to work in factories

So by the beginning of the twentieth century, young children were no longer allowed to work in factories, and women were limited to ten hours a day. Things had come a long way since the early days when long hours, even for the youngest children, were considered quite normal.

Work it out!

1 Why do you think the owners of the factories preferred to use women and children? Explain your answer as fully as you can.

2 From this chapter, find as many examples as you can of dangers or hardships faced by women and children in factories in Victorian times. Explain why they were dangerous.

3 A museum of industrial history is preparing a display on child and women workers in the factories. It is called:

'A very hard and dangerous life.'

You are preparing a leaflet that will go with the display. You will need no more than one sheet of A4 but it can be folded as many times as you like. You will need to include text, pictures, personal stories and personal profiles. Don't forget you are trying to attract visitors to the museum.

4 Why do you think that very few factory owners were willing to follow Robert Owen's example?

An ever-increasing Empire: British expansion 1750–1900

In 1900, Britain controlled just under a quarter of the entire world and ruled just over a fifth of the people. Queen Victoria was the head of the largest Empire in the history of the world and ruled over 400 million people. How had a small nation come to control so much of the world?

Worldwide land grabbing

Britain first began to gain an Empire early in the seventeenth century, when British settlers landed on the east coast of America and founded **colonies** such as Pennsylvania and Massachusetts. Later, in 1664, New Amsterdam was seized from the Dutch and renamed 'New York'.

Britain also gained colonies in the Caribbean. Jamaica was the first colony won by force in 1655 and, together with St Kitts, Barbados and several other small islands, provided a valuable base for the profitable sugar trade. Nearer to home, Britain had also gained the territories of Gibraltar (1704) and Minorca (1708), after defeating the Spanish in war.

In 1763, Britain beat the French in the Seven Years' War. This war had been fought largely over who should control foreign territories. During the war, Robert Clive won a great victory over the French at Plassey in 1757, laying the foundations for the British later to gain complete

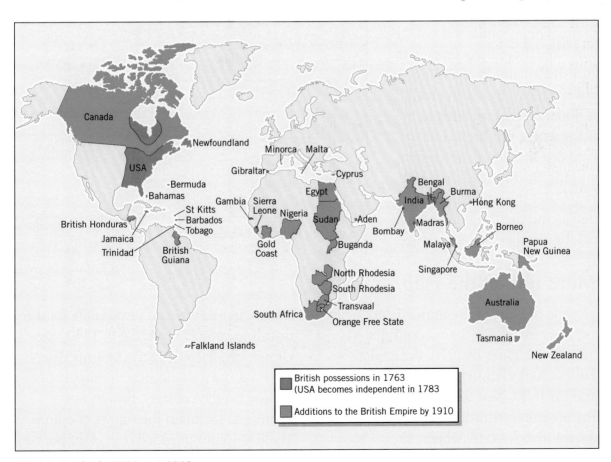

Britain's Empire in 1763 and 1910.

control of India. In the same period, James Wolfe launched an all-out attack on the French in Canada. Wolfe's great victory capturing Quebec in 1763 meant complete control of Canada for Britain. These successes provoked great enthusiasm for 'Empire-building' in Britain. The first steps had been taken in building the mighty British Empire.

The American colonies break free

By 1750, Britain owned thirteen colonies on the eastern coast of America. The British government expected these colonies to pay taxes to help towards the cost of running them. The colonists did not see why they should pay taxes to the British Parliament when they did not have any say in electing it. Relations deteriorated to the point where war broke out between the American colonies and the British in 1775. Eight years later the British accepted defeat and the thirteen colonies celebrated their independence.

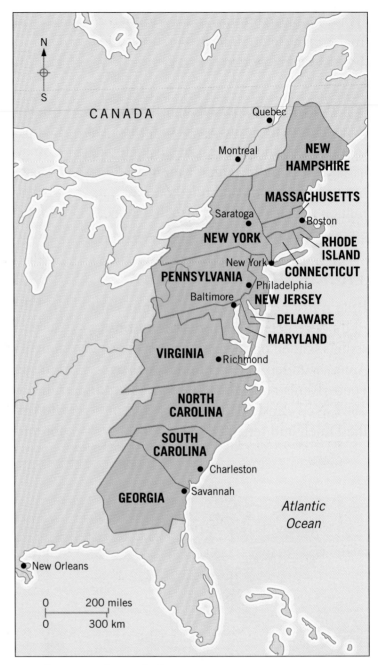

The thirteen American colonies.

More red on the map

Despite the loss of the thirteen American colonies in 1783, Britain continued to build its Empire. In 1770, the explorer James Cook claimed Australia for Britain and, in 1840, New Zealand became a British colony. Further victories in India meant that, by 1900, almost the whole of the country was under British control.

Victory in war was also responsible for the British gaining Hong Kong in 1842, after China was defeated in the Opium War. This was not a war to stop the supply of **opium**; on the contrary, Britain was fighting to maintain the supply of opium. Trading opium provided over eight per cent of Britain's total overseas trade in 1833.

This demonstrates how trade was often a major consideration in Britain's plans to increase the Empire.

An increase in trade was also behind Stamford Raffles claiming Singapore for the British in 1819. He was told to find a base in south-east Asia which would enable Britain to carry on its rich trade with China, without having to pay taxes to use Dutch-owned ports. By the end of the nineteenth century Britain had extended its influence from Singapore to control almost all of Malaya as well.

Source A

We have to remember that it is part of our heritage to take care that (as far as it can be) the world is shaped by us. It must receive an English speaking character and not that of other nations.

Lord Rosebery, British Foreign Secretary, speaking in 1893.

The scramble for Africa

Britain played a major part in what became known as 'the scramble for Africa'. By 1850, the British had gained Cape Colony (South Africa) from the Dutch and were also in control of Egypt. During the nineteenth century the British began trying to win greater control over the whole of the southern part of Africa. These efforts were encouraged by the chance of great riches that the recently discovered gold and diamond mines could bring. Cecil Rhodes, Prime Minister of the Cape Colony, had a dream. He wished for Britain to rule a stretch of land from the Cape in South Africa to Cairo in Egypt, in the north of Africa. In the 1880s and 1890s his dream came true, as 80 per cent of Africa was divided up between the nations of Europe. Britain took control of sixteen colonies.

Reasons why the British built an Empire

1 **It happened by mistake!** Sometimes territories came Britain's way as a result of wars fought for other reasons, e.g. Gibraltar in 1704.

2 **Trade.** Most colonies were established because they were valuable as trade bases, e.g. Singapore in 1819. Sometimes the colonies themselves had valuable raw materials or spices.

3 **Strategic positions.** Some colonies were on important sea routes or provided excellent bases for defence. For instance, Gibraltar guarded the entrance to the Mediterranean Sea, and this gave the British a lot of control of who went in and out.

4 **'The White Man's Burden'.** Many Europeans considered that their culture and civilisation was superior to that of other continents. It was therefore necessary to colonise areas to 'civilise' the local people. In particular, this meant teaching them Christianity.

5 **To stop rivals becoming more powerful.** The nineteenth century saw the rapid expansion of colonies by a number of European powers. Britain had to make sure that her rivals, such as France and Germany, did not gain colonies at British expense.

6 **Popular enthusiasm.** At times the British government was responding to enthusiasm for Empire-building amongst the ordinary people of Britain. This was particularly true after 1870.

By the time of Queen Victoria's Diamond Jubilee in 1897, many people in Britain believed they were part of an Empire that would never end. The phrase they used was 'an Empire where the sun never sets.' Events in the twentieth century were to prove them wrong.

GOVERNOR DAVEY'S
PROCLAMATION
TO THE ABORIGINES
1816.

"Why Massa Gubernor", said Black Jack.. "You Proclamation all gammon"
"How blackfellow read him eh? He no learn him read book."
"Read that then" said the Governor: pointing to a picture.

A poster issued by the British Governor of Tasmania, Australia. The British first landed in Tasmania in 1803. This poster was designed to show that the local black population and white settlers would receive the same treatment. By 1876, however, the black population had been wiped out.

Work it out!

1 You've been asked to make a contribution to a programme on the radio about why Britain gained an Empire. You have 20 seconds only to make your points. What would you say?

2 The Victorians were very proud of the British Empire. Do you think we would feel as proud today if Britain still had a large Empire? Explain your answer as fully as you can.

3 What do you think is meant by the phrase, an 'Empire upon which the sun never sets'? Do you think this is a good description of the British Empire? Why?

Glossary

abolition/abolish do away with completely (customs, practices, institutions) sometimes by a new law being passed.

Act of Parliament law created and approved by both Houses of Parliament and signed by the monarch. It is binding on every person in the United Kingdom.

anaesthetic substance used in medicine to make you unconscious, usually to protect a patient from the pain of an operation.

barber someone who cuts men's hair.

Barnardos charitable homes for orphaned children started by Dr Barnardo at the end of the nineteenth century.

Board of Health before cholera arrived in England in 1831 the government set up a central committee (board) in London to raise money to improve water supplies and drainage in the slums. Local boards of health were also created in districts with a high death rate.

census official numbering of the population with regard to various statistics.

cholera contagious and often fatal disease bringing violent sickness and diarrhoea.

colony a region or land claimed by a European country, and either occupied by settlers from that country or governed by a few representatives of the mother country for the purposes of trade or war.

commute to travel some distance to and from work every day, usually by public transport.

contagious (diseases) diseases which are passed from one person to another by physical contact.

Corporation of the Poor a committee responsible for collecting money to look after the poor and improve living conditions.

court a yard enclosed all round with buildings and only a passage way to the street (see page 49).

domestic system the way the making of goods was organised, not in factories but in the houses of the workers and craftsmen.

drudgery long hours of work in poor conditions for little money.

entrepreneur a go-ahead business man willing to back new ideas and take risks.

epidemic widespread outbreak of a disease in a community at a particular time.

evangelical a protestant group who believed that preaching the Gospel of Christ was the most important part of the Anglican religion.

fraternity a group closely drawn together for reasons of religion or friendship.

gynaecology the medical study of women's bodies.

hewers miners who used picks at the coal-face to hack out the coal.

illiterate unable to read or write.

immune safe from, untouched by (disease).

obstetrics the medical study of childbirth.

offal rubbish and waste from dead animals and food. Some of this is still edible, like the intestines, liver or kidneys of animals.

opium an addictive drug made from poppies and widely used and smoked in 'opium dens'. Also used as a painkiller in medicine.

Peterloo the mass reform meeting at St Peter's Fields, Manchester, in 1819, which was broken up by the troops and 11 people died.

Privy Council the inner council of advisers to the king/queen, which became very powerful during Henry VIII's reign. By the nineteenth century it was larger and less powerful.

Salvation Army 'General' Booth's organisation for the revival of religion among the industrial working classes. Salvation Army brass bands were frequently heard playing in the streets.

sanitation state of cleanliness, particularly in connection with water supplies and sewage disposal.

slavery when one person is bought by and belongs to another person. The slave is then completely under the control of the 'master' and owes him total obedience.

status quo the existing state of affairs.

Temperance Group a society who opposed and tried to ban the drinking of alcohol throughout the country.

toll a charge made at a turnpike or tollgate for using a privately owned road.

vested interests a description of people who have an 'interest' – ie have invested money in an existing business or set-up, or have the right to make money from an existing situation.